Vintage Knit Hats

21 Patterns for Timeless Fashions

Kathryn Fulton

Photographs by Alan Wycheck and Tiffany Blackstone

STACKPOLE
BOOKS

Published by
STACKPOLE BOOKS
5067 Ritter Road
Mechanicsburg, PA 17055
www.stackpolebooks.com

Printed in the United States of America

10 9 8 7 6 5 4 3 2

First edition

Cover design by Tessa J. Sweigert
All photos by Alan Wychek except as indicated.
Photos by Tiffany Blackstone: Pages 1, 3 (bottom), 35,
37 (bottom), 42, 45, 49, 59, 62, 65, 69, 72.

Library of Congress Cataloging-in-Publication Data

Fulton, Kathryn, 1987–
  Vintage knit hats : 21 patterns for timeless fashions /
Kathryn Fulton. —
First edition.
    pages cm
  ISBN 978-0-8117-1142-5
1. Knitting—Patterns. 2. Hats. 3. Caps (Headgear) I. Title.
  TT825.F85 2013
  746.43'2—dc23
                    2013023540

Contents

Rose Cloche

Step back to the 1920s with this simple but feminine cloche. The brim shaping is done with short rows—which can be a challenge for beginners—but once you're past the brim this hat knits up fast, with bulky weight yarn and big needles. Be sure to sew the ribbon on loosely to allow the hat to stretch.

5

Bulky

YARN
Bernat Alpaca Chunky Yarn
(70% acyrlic, 30% alpaca;
120 yd/110 m; 3.5 oz/100 g)
in tomato (1 skein)

NEEDLES
1 set size 13/9 mm straight needles *or size
needed to obtain gauge*

NOTIONS
Yarn needle
Ribbon (1¼" wide)
Sewing thread to match the ribbon

MEASUREMENTS
Circumference at edge of flared brim 30"

GAUGE
11 sts = 4" / 7 rows = 2"

PATTERN

BRIM
Cast on 41 sts.

Row 1: Increasing as to purl, inc 1 st in each of first 7 sts, p1; *inc 1 st in next st, p1; repeat from * 12 times, inc. 1 st in each of last 7 sts. (68 sts)

Row 2: K20, turn.

Row 3: Slip 1, p19.

Row 4: K all sts.

Row 5: P20, turn.

Row 6: Slip 1, k19.

Row 7: Purl.

Row 8: Knit.

Rows 9–10: Repeat rows 7–8.

Row 11: Knit tbl across. (Turning ridge)

Row 12: Knit.

Row 13: Purl.

Rows 14–17: Repeat rows 12–13 twice.

Row 18: K2, k2tog, [k1, k2tog] 5 times, k2tog 16 times, [k1, k2tog] 5 times, k2. (41 sts)

Mark for beginning of crown.

Row 19: Purl.

Row 20: Knit.

Row 21: P2; *pfb, p4; repeat from * to last 4 sts; pfb, p3. (49 sts)

Work in stockinette stitch until 5 ins above marker for beginning of crown. End with a purl row.

Decrease row 1: K1, *ssk, k4, k2tog; repeat from * to end. (37 sts)

Work 3 rows even.

Decrease row 2: K1, *ssk, k2, t2tog; repeat from * to end. (25 sts)

Work 1 row even.

Decrease row 3: K1, *ssk, k2tog; repeat from * to end. (13 sts)

Cut yarn and draw through remaining loops.

FINISHING
Sew the back seam. Turn under the bottom of the hem along the turning ridge and sew cast-on row loosely to brim decrease row. Weave in ends.

With sewing thread, sew the ribbon around the hat just above the edge of the flaring brim. Be careful to leave enough slack in the ribbon to allow the hat to stretch to fit.

Floppy Tam

SKILL LEVEL

BEGINNER

Nothing could be simpler than this stylish garter-stitch tam—you don't even need to know how to purl! The first 10 rows are worked on smaller needles to create the band; be sure to keep your tension nice and tight on these rows for a snug fit. You can ease up on the tension in the main part of the hat.

4

Medium

YARN
Pattons Classic Wool (100% pure new wool; 210 yd/192 m; 3.5 oz/100 g) in leaf green (1 skein)

NEEDLES
1 set each size 4/3.5 mm and 8/5 mm straight needles *or size needed to obtain gauge*

NOTIONS
Yarn needle

MEASUREMENTS
Circumference at brim (unstretched) 25"; diameter (hat laid flat) 12"

GAUGE
In garter stitch with size 8 needles, 4 sts / 7 rows = 1"

PATTERN

With smaller needles, cast on 108 sts. Work even in garter st for 10 rows.

With size 8 needles, continue to work in garter st until piece measures 7 1/4 inches.

Decrease row 1: K3tog across row. (36 sts)

Row 2: Knit.

Row 3: Repeat row 1. (12 sts)

Row 4: Knit.

Cut yarn; draw end through remaining 12 sts tightly. Fasten securely.

POMPOM

Wind yarn 180 times around a piece of cardboard 3 inches wide. Tie the loops securely at one end; cut the other end. Trim to desired size.

FINISHING

Sew back seam and weave in ends. Sew pompom to crown of hat.

Merry Tasseled Hat

This festive hat will keep kids' heads warm during sleigh rides and snowball fights. Try it in a different color combination for a hat to wear all winter long!

YARN
Knit Picks Swish DK (100% superwash merino wool; 123 yd; 50 g)

A: jade (1 skein)
B: white (1 skein)
C: hollyberry (1 skein)

NEEDLES
1 set size 8/5 mm circular or double-pointed needles *or size needed to obtain gauge*
Size G-6/4 mm crochet hook

MEASUREMENTS
Circumference at brim 17" (unstretched); full length (with brim not turned up and tip not folded over) 16"

GAUGE
5 sts / 6 rows = 1"

CROCHET STITCH USED
Chain (ch)

PATTERN

With color A, cast on 84 sts (28 sts on each needle).
    Join to work in round, placing marker at beg of
    round. Work in k1, p1 ribbing for 5 inches.
    Continue in stockinette st (i.e., knit all rounds).
    Work 2 rounds in color B.
Follow chart for next 16 rounds.
Rounds 17–20: Knit with color B.
Rounds 21–23: Repeat rounds 11–13.
Round 24: With color B, *k1, k2tog, k36, k2tog, k1.
    Repeat from * once more. (80 sts)
Round 25: Knit.
Round 26: *K1, k2tog, k34, k2tog, k1. Repeat from *
    once more. (76 sts)
Round 27: Knit.

Round 28: *K1, k2tog, k32, k2tog, k1. Repeat from *
    once more. (72 sts)
Round 29: Knit.
Round 30: *K1, k2tog, k30, k2tog, k1. Repeat from *
    once more. (68 sts)
Round 31: Knit.
Round 32: *K1, k2tog, k28, k2tog, k1. Repeat from *
    once more. (64 sts)
Round 33: Knit.
Rounds 34–36: Repeat rounds 11–13.
Round 37: With color B, *k1, k2tog, k26, k2tog, k1.
    Repeat from * once more. (60 sts)
Round 38: Knit.
Round 39: *K1, k2tog, k24, k2tog, k1. Repeat from *
    once more. (56 sts)
Round 40: Knit.
Round 42: *K1, k2tog, k22, k2tog, k1. Repeat from *
    once more. (52 sts)
Round 43: Knit.
Round 44: *K1, k2tog, k20, k2tog, k1. Repeat from *
    once more. (48 sts)
Round 45: Knit.
Round 46: *K1, k2tog, k18, k2tog, k1. Repeat from *
    once more. (44 sts)
Rounds 47–49: Repeat rounds 11–13.
Round 50: With color B, *k1, k2tog, k16, k2tog, k1.
    Repeat from * once more. (40 sts)
Round 51: *K1, k2tog, k14, k2tog, k1. Repeat from *
    once more. (36 sts)
Round 52: *K1, k2tog, k12, k2tog, k1. Repeat from *
    once more. (32 sts)

Round 53: *K1, k2tog, k10, k2tog, k1. Repeat from *
once more. (28 sts)

Round 54: *K1, k2tog, k8, k2tog, k1. Repeat from *
once more. (24 sts)

Round 55: *K1, k2tog, k6, k2tog, k1. Repeat from *
once more. (20 sts)

Round 56: *K1, k2tog, k4, k2tog, k1. Repeat from *
once more. (16 sts)

Round 57: *K1, k2tog, k2, k2tog, k1. Repeat from *
once more. (12 sts)

Round 58: *K1, k2tog, k2tog, k1. Repeat from * once
more. (8 sts)

Thread yarn through remaining sts and fasten off
securely.

FINISHING

Weave in ends. Using 2 strands of color C, crochet a
2½-inch chain. Make a tassel and sew one end of
the chain to the tassel and the other end to the top
of the cap. Fold over the top of the hat and tack it
to the row immediately above the ribbing.

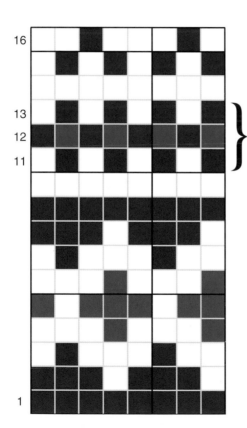

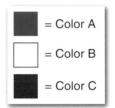

= Color A

= Color B

= Color C

Rounds 11–13
Repeat these rounds for
rounds 21–23, 34–36, and 47–49

Popcorn Pompom Hat

SKILL LEVEL

INTERMEDIATE

This playful topper for toddlers and younger kids will keep little cheeks and ears warm with style. The construction is a little unusual—you begin with the strap, adding the earflaps next and finally the body of the hat—but the knitting is straightforward. A subtle pattern of knits and purls adds texture.

4
Medium

YARN
Knit Picks Swish Worsted
(100% superwash merino wool;
110 yd; 50 g) in parrot (2 skeins)

NEEDLES
1 set size 7/4.5 mm straight needles *or size needed to obtain gauge*

NOTIONS
Yarn needle

MEASUREMENTS
Circumference at brim (unstretched) 18"

GAUGE
In pattern, 5 sts / 7 rows = 1"

PATTERN

STRAP

Cast on 2 sts.
Row 1: Inc in first st, k1.
Row 2: K1, p1, k1.
Row 3: Inc in each of first 2 sts, k1.
Row 4: K1, p3, k1.
Row 5: K1, inc in each of next 2 sts, k2.
Row 6: K1, p1, k1, yo, k2tog, p1, k1.
Row 7: K2, [p1, k1] twice, k1.
Row 8: [K1, p1] 3 times, k1.
Repeat rows 7–8 until strap measures 4³⁄₄ inches, finishing with a row 8.

FIRST EARFLAP

The first earflap is worked as a continuation of the strap.

Row 1: K2, p1, inc twice in next st, p1, k2.
Row 2: K1, p1, p to last 3 sts, k1, p1, k1.
Row 3: K2, p1, inc in each of next 2 sts, k1, p1, k2.
Row 4: Repeat row 2.
Row 5: K2, p1, inc in next st; knit to last 5 sts; inc in next st, k1, p1, k2.
Row 6: Repeat row 2.
Row 7: K2, p1, inc in next st; *k1, p1; repeat from * to last 5 sts; inc in next st, k1, p1, k2.
Row 8: Repeat row 2.
Rows 9–16: Repeat rows 5–8.
Row 17: K2, p1, k to last 3 sts, p1, k2.
Cut yarn. Slip these 23 sts onto a length of scrap yarn and set them aside.

SECOND EARFLAP

Cast on 7 sts.
Preliminary row 1: K2, [p1, k1] twice, k1.
Preliminary row 2: [K1, p1] 3 times, k1.
Continue as with first earflap, starting with Row 1.

BODY OF HAT

Cast on 12 sts. Slip 23 sts of first earflap onto empty needle; with wrong side of work facing, k1, p1, k1, p17, k1, p1, k1 across these sts. Cast on 31 sts. Work across second earflap as the first. Cast on 12 sts. (101 sts)
Row 1: K1, *p1, k1; repeat from * to last st, k1.
Row 2: [K1, p1] 7 times, k1, p17, *k1, p1; repeat from * to last 33 sts, k1, p17, [k1, p1] 7 times, k1.
Row 3: K2, [p1, k1] 7 times, k16, [p1, k1] 18 times, p1, k17, [p1, k1] 7 times, k1.
Row 4: Repeat row 2.
Row 5: Repeat row 1.
Row 6: K1, p to last st, k1.
Row 7: Knit.
Row 8: Repeat row 6.
Rows 9–32: Repeat rows 5–8.

CROWN

Row 1: K1, [k7, k2tog] 11 times, k1. (90 sts)
Row 2: K1, p to last st, k1.
Row 3: K1, [k6, k2tog] 11 times, k1. (79 sts)
Row 4: Repeat row 2.
Row 5: K1, [k5, k2tog] 11 times, k1. (68 sts)
Row 6: Repeat row 2.
Row 7: K1, [k4, k2tog] 11 times, k1. (57 sts)
Row 8: Repeat row 2.
Row 9: K1, [k3, k2tog] 11 times, k1. (46 sts)
Row 10: Repeat row 2.
Row 11: K1, [k2, k2tog] 11 times, k1. (35 sts)
Row 12: Repeat row 2.
Row 13: K1, [k1, k2tog] 11 times, k1. (24 sts)
Row 14: Repeat row 2.
Row 15: K1, k2tog 11 times, k1. (13 sts)
Cut yarn. Draw end through remaining sts
    and fasten off.

FINISHING

Sew back seam. To make pompom, wrap yarn
around a piece of carboard 1 1/2 inches wide 200
times. Tie the strands of yarn firmly together at one
edge; cut the strands at the opposite edge. Trim the
pompom and sew to crown of hat. Sew a button on
the earflap without the strap. Weave in ends.

Berries and Cream Ski Cap

Knitted in a loose gauge in soft 100% wool, this hat is deliciously soft and fluffy. The color pattern is worked with slipped stitches so you never have to carry more than one strand of yarn at a time.

YARN
Cascade Yarns Eco + (100%
Peruvian highland wool;
478 yd/237 m; 8.75 oz/250 g)
A: 8010 (natural) (1 skein)
B: 6915 (pink) (1 skein)
C: 0508 (purple) (1 skein)

NEEDLES
1 set size 10/6 mm straight needles *or size
    needed to obtain gauge*

NOTIONS
Yarn needle

MEASUREMENTS
Circumference at brim (unstretched) 21"

GAUGE
In pattern, 3 sts / 6 rows = 1"

PATTERN

With A, cast on 20 sts.
Row 1: Purl.
Row 2: Inc in every st across. (40 sts)
Row 3: Purl.
Row 4: K1, kfb in next st and in every st across.
   (79 sts)
Row 5: Purl.
Row 6: Knit.
Row 7: Purl.
Row 8: With B, k3; *with yarn at back of work, slip 1
   st as to p, k3; repeat from * to end.
Row 9: With B, k3; *with yarn at front of work, slip 1
   st as to p, k3; repeat from * to end.
Row 10: With A, k1; *with yarn at back of work, slip 1
   st as to p, k3; repeat from * to last 2 sts; with yarn
   at back, slip 1 st as to p, k1.
Row 11: With A, k1, *with yarn at front of work, slip 1
   st as to p, k3; repeat from * to last 2 sts; with yarn
   at front, slip 1 st as to p, k1.
Row 12: With A, knit.
Row 13: With A, purl.
Rows 14–31: Repeat the 6 rows of the pattern (rows
   8–13) 3 times.
Row 32: With A, purl.
Row 33: With A, knit.
Row 34: With A, knit.
Rows 35–64: Repeat the 6 rows of the pattern (row
   8–13) 5 times. The wrong side of the work will be
   on the opposite side from before (this is for the
   turned brim).
Row 65: With C, work row 8.
Row 66: With C, work row 9.
Bind off.

POMPOM

Wind C 70 times around a piece of cardboard 3 in.
wide. Tie the loops securely at one end; cut the
other end. Trim to desired size.

FINISHING

Sew the back seam, matching up the stripes. With a
yarn needle, draw a strand of yarn through the 20
sts of the cast-on edge, gather them tightly, and
fasten securely. Weave in ends. Sew pompom to
crown of hat.

Cabled Watch Cap

This classic cap for men or women is knitted with fine yarn on small needles for a dense, warm fabric. You can adjust the height of the hat—make it shorter for a smaller head or longer to be worn as a slouchy beanie—by adding or removing a cable twist.

YARN
Knit Picks City Tweed DK (55% merino wool, 25% superfine alpaca, 20% donegal tweed; 123 yd; 50 g) in Habanero (2 skeins)

NEEDLES
1 set each size 3/3.25 mm and 6/4 mm double-pointed needles *or size needed to obtain gauge*

NOTIONS
Cable needle

MEASUREMENTS
Circumference at brim (unstretched) 16"; height from turned brim to crown 9$\frac{1}{2}$"

GAUGE
With larger needles, 11 sts = 2"; 8 rounds = 1"

SPECIAL STITCH
Cable 8 back (C8B): Slip next 4 sts onto a cable needle. Hold the needle at the back of the work. Knit the next 4 stitches from the left-hand needle, then knit the 4 stitches from the cable needle.

PATTERN

With larger needles, cast on 120 sts.
Work 5$\frac{1}{2}$ inches in k1, p1 ribbing. Switch to smaller
   needles and proceed:
Round 1: *K10, p1, k8, p1. Repeat from * to end of
   round.
Rounds 2–4: Repeat round 1.
Round 5: *K10, p1, C8B, p1. Repeat from * to end of
   round.
Rounds 6–8: Repeat round 1.
Repeat rounds 1–8 three times.

CROWN SHAPING
Round 1: *K2tog five times, p1, k8, p1. Repeat from *
   to end of round. (90 sts)
Round 2: *K5, p1, k8, p1. Repeat from * to end of
   round.
Rounds 3–4: Repeat round 2.
Round 5: *K5, p1, C8B, p1. Repeat from * to end of
   round.
Rounds 6–8: Repeat rounds 2–4.
Round 9: *K3tog, k2tog, p1, k8, p1. Repeat from * to
   end of round. (72 sts)
Round 10: *K2, p1, k8, p1. Repeat from * to end of
   round.
Rounds 11–12: Repeat round 10.
Round 13: *P3tog, C8B, p1. Repeat from * to end of
   round. (60 sts)
Round 14: *P1, k8, p1. Repeat from * to end of
   round.
Round 15: Repeat round 14.
Round 16: *K2tog, k6, k2tog. Repeat from * to end
   of round.
Rounds 17–19: Work in k1, p1 ribbing.
Round 20: K2tog 24 times.
Cut yarn, draw end through rem sts, pull tightly,
   and fasten off. Weave in ends.

Angora Beret

Angora yarn makes a lightweight but very warm hat. We've included instructions for a youth and child size—since if you make one, you may get requests for more!

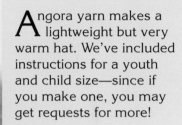

YARN
Louisa Harding Yarns Kimono Angora Pure (70% angora, 25% wool, 5% nylon; 125 yd/114 m; 25 g) in #6 (blue) (2 skeins)

NEEDLES
1 set size 8/5 mm straight needles *or size needed to obtain gauge*

NOTIONS
Yarn needle

MEASUREMENTS
Ladies: Circumference at brim (unstretched) 21"; diameter $10\frac{1}{2}$"
Youth: Circumference at brim $19\frac{1}{2}$"; diameter $9\frac{1}{2}$"
Child: Circumference at brim 18"; diameter $8\frac{1}{2}$"

GAUGE
7 sts / 9 rows = 1" (in stockinette st)

PATTERN

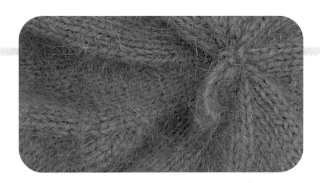

**Instructions are written for ladies' size.
Instructions for youth size and child size
are in brackets {Youth; Child}.**

BODY OF HAT

Cast on 94 {88; 80} sts loosely.
Row 1: *K1, p1. Repeat from * to end.
Rows 2–8: Repeat row 1.

**Ribbed band should easily stretch
to measure 22 {21½; 21} inches.**

Row 9 **(ladies' size):** [K1, p1] twice. *K1, M1, p1. [K1,
p1] eight times. Repeat from * to end of row.
(99 sts)
Row 9 **(youth size):** [K1, p1] eleven times, M1, [k1,
p1] twenty-two times, M1, [k1, p1] eleven times.
(90 sts)
Row 9 **(child's size):** Repeat row 1. (80 sts)
Row 10: K1, p to last st, k1.
Row 11: *K9 {k9; k8}, M1. Repeat from * to end of
row. (110 sts {100 sts; 90 sts;})
Row 12: Repeat row 10.
Row 13: *K10 {k10; k9}, M1. Repeat from * to end of
row. (121 sts {110 sts; 100 sts})
Row 14: Repeat row 10.
Row 15: *K11 {k11; k10}, M1. Repeat from * to end of
row. (132 sts {120 sts; 110 sts})
Row 16: Repeat row 10.
Row 17: *K12 {k12; k11}, M1. Repeat from * to end of
row. (143 sts {130 sts; 120 sts})
Row 18: Repeat row 10.
Row 19: *K13 {k13; k12}, M1. Repeat from * to end of
row. (154 sts {140 sts; 130 sts})
Row 20: Repeat row 10.

Row 21: *K14 {k14; k13}, M1. Repeat from * to end of
row. (165 sts {150 sts; 140 sts})
Row 22: Repeat row 10.
Row 23: *K15 {k15; k14}, M1. Repeat from * to end of
row. (176 sts {160 sts; 150 sts})
Row 24: Repeat row 10.
Row 25: *K16 {k16; k15}, M1. Repeat from * to end of
row. (187 sts {170 sts; 160 sts})
Row 26: Repeat row 10.
Row 27: *K17 {k17; k16}, M1. Repeat from * to end of
row. (198 sts {180 sts; 170 sts})
Work 21 rows {13 rows; 5 rows} in stockinette st,
beginning and ending with a purl row.

CROWN SHAPING

Row 1: *K16 {k16; k15}, k2tog. Repeat from * to end
of row. (187 sts {170 sts; 160 sts})
Row 2: K1, p to last st, k1.
Row 3: *K15 {k15; k14}, k2tog. Repeat from * to end
of row. (176 sts {160 sts; 150 sts})
Row 4: Repeat row 2.
Row 5: *K14 {k14; k13}, k2tog. Repeat from * to end
of row. (165 sts {150 sts; 140 sts})
Row 6: Repeat row 2.
Row 7: *K13 {k13; k12}, k2tog. Repeat from * to end
of row. (154 sts {140 sts; 130 sts})
Row 8: Repeat row 2.
Row 9: *K12 {k12; k11}, k2tog. Repeat from * to end
of row. (143 sts {130 sts; 120 sts})
Row 10: Repeat row 2.
Row 11: *K11 {k11; k10}, k2tog. Repeat from * to end
of row. (132 sts {120 sts; 110 sts})

Row 12: Repeat row 2.

Row 13: *K10 {k10; k9}, k2tog. Repeat from * to end of row. (121 sts {110 sts; 100 sts})

Row 14: Repeat row 2.

Row 15: *K9 {k9; k8}, k2tog. Repeat from * to end of row. (110 sts {100 sts; 90 sts})

Row 16: Repeat row 2.

Row 17: *K9 {k9; k8}, k2tog. Repeat from * to end of row. (99 sts {90 sts; 80 sts})

Row 18: Repeat row 2.

Row 19: *K8 {k8; k7}, k2tog. Repeat from * to end of row. (88 sts {80 sts; 70 sts})

Row 20: Repeat row 2.

Row 21: *K7 {k7; k6}, k2tog. Repeat from * to end of row. (77 sts {70 sts; 60 sts})

Row 22: Repeat row 2.

Row 23: *K6 {k6; k5}, k2tog. Repeat from * to end of row. (66 sts {60 sts; 50 sts})

Row 24: Repeat row 2.

Row 25: *K5 {k5; k4}, k2tog. Repeat from * to end of row. (55 sts {50 sts; 40 sts})

Row 26: Repeat row 2.

Row 27: *K4 {k4; k3}, k2tog. Repeat from * to end of row. (44 sts {40 sts; 30 sts})

Row 28: Repeat row 2.

Row 29: *K3 {k3; k2}, k2tog. Repeat from * to end of row. (33 sts {30 sts; 20 sts})

Youth size: Skip to last row now.

Row 30: Repeat row 2.

Row 31: *K2 {k2; —}, k2tog. Repeat from * to end of row. (22 sts {20 sts; —})

Last row **(all sizes):** *P2tog. Repeat from * to end of row. (11 sts {10 sts; 10 sts})

Cut yarn, draw end through remaining loops.

FINISHING

Sew seam. If desired, a piece of heavy ribbon may be sewn on the inside of the ribbed band. Weave in ends.

Leave tam plain or trim with a pompom or tab. (To make tab, cast on 6 sts loosely with two strands of yarn held together; bind off loosely and sew both ends to top of beret.)

Striped Hood

Hat and scarf in one, this hood is a longer knit—but the changing ribbing pattern and the stripes will keep the knitting interesting. Or use heavier-weight yarn and bigger needles for a quick, bulky hood.

Medium

YARN
Pattons Classic Wool (100%
pure new wool; 210 yd/192 m;
100 g/3.5 oz)
A: chestnut brown (1 skein)
B: jade heather (1 skein)

NEEDLES
1 set size 8/5 mm straight needles *or size
    needed to obtain gauge*

NOTIONS
Yarn needle

MEASUREMENTS
Length of one side of scarf from top of head
    to end of scarf (excluding fringe) 30"

GAUGE
In pattern, 5 sts / 7 rows = 1"

PATTERN

With A, cast on 46 sts.

NARROW STRIPE
Row 1 (WS): *K1, p1; repeat from * to end.
Rows 2–7: Repeat row 1.
Row 8: *P1, k1; repeat from * to end.
Rows 9–14: Repeat row 8.

WIDE STRIPE
With B, work rows 1–14 twice; 28 rows in all.
Repeat narrow stripes in A and wide stripes in B
    alternately until there are 10 narrow stripes and
    9 wide stripes (end with a narrow stripe). Bind
    off in ribbing.

FRINGE
Wind B 138 times around a 5-inch piece of
cardboard. Cut along one edge of the wraps. Knot 3
strands in every other stitch along each end of the
scarf. Trim the ends evenly.

FINISHING
Fold scarf at the center, with the ends meeting.
With matching colors, sew the seam for the back of
the hood, sewing for 8 inches and matching up the
stripes. Weave in ends.

Hunter Cap

The dark earth tones and tie-free earflaps on this hat make it grown-up enough to satisfy an older boy—but you could substitute brighter colors for a younger child. The single-crochet edging gives the hat a nice finish, but it can be omitted if desired.

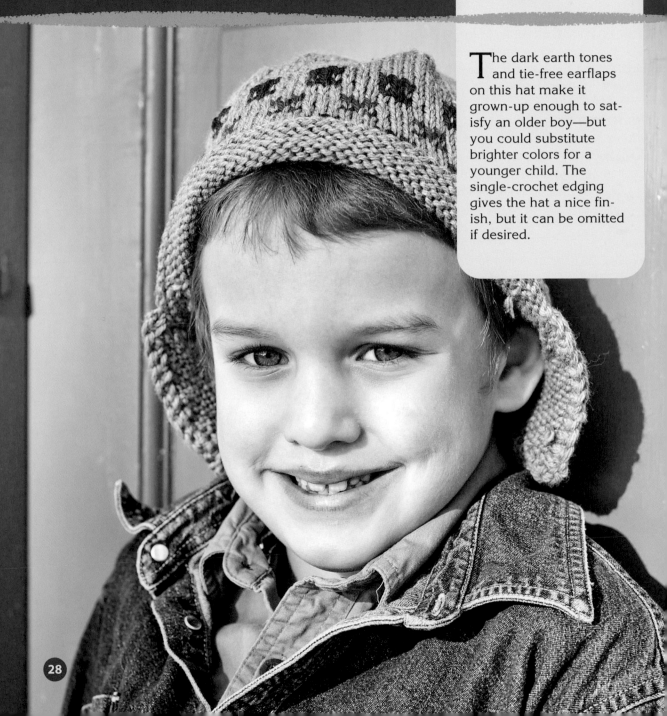

YARN
Knit Picks Swish DK (100%
superwash merino wool;
123 yd; 50 g)
A: squirrel heather (2 skeins)
B: bark (1 skein)
C: jade (1 skein)

NEEDLES
1 set size 4/3.5 mm double-pointed needles
   or size needed to obtain gauge
Size H/8 (5.0 mm) crochet hook

MEASUREMENTS
Circumference at brim (unstretched) 21"

GAUGE
5 st / 7 rows = 1"

CROCHET STITCH USED
Single crochet (sc)

PATTERN

With color A, cast on 102 sts and work in garter st
for 6 rounds. Change to stockinette stitch and
continue until the work measures 1¹/₂ inches
from the beginning, ending with a purl row.

Follow the chart for the next 13 rows. Decrease 2
sts at the end of the last row. (100 sts)

Continue in stockinette st in color A until piece
measures 4³/₄ inches from beginning, finishing
with a purl row.

Dec row 1: *Ssk, k18, k2tog; repeat from * to end of
row. (90 sts)

Dec row 2 and every even row: Purl.

Dec row 3: *Ssk, k16, k2tog; repeat from * to end of
row. (80 sts)

Dec row 5: *Ssk, k14, k2tog; repeat from * to end of
row. (70 sts)

Dec row 7: *Ssk, k12, k2tog; repeat from * to end of
row. (60 sts)

Dec row 9: *Ssk, k10, k2tog; repeat from * to end of
row. (50 sts)

Dec row 11: *Ssk, k8, k2tog; repeat from * to end of
row. (40 sts)

Dec row 13: *Ssk, k6, k2tog; repeat from * to end of
row. (30 sts)

Cut yarn and draw end through remaining sts.
Fasten off.

EARFLAPS

With the right side of the work toward you, using
color A, pick up and knit 22 sts along the bottom
edge of the hat, starting 5 sts past the center of
the back of the hat (where your first row was
joined to make a round).

Rows 1–4: Knit.

Row 5: Ssk, knit to last 2 sts, k2tog.

Row 6: Knit.

Repeat rows 5–6 until 2 sts remain. K2tog and
fasten off.

Make the second earflap in the same way.

FINISHING

Using a crochet hook, work a single row of single
crochet around the edges of both earflaps. Weave
in ends.

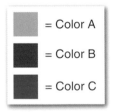

= Color A

= Color B

= Color C

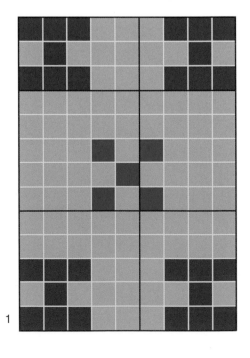

1

City Stocking Cap

This classic stocking cap is fast to make and very warm. The turned brim incorporates twists (also called mock cables) for a stylish look that is very easy to knit.

4
Medium

YARN
Merino-acrylic blend worsted-weight yarn in gray (3 skeins)

NEEDLES
1 set size 4/3.5 mm straight needles *or size needed to obtain gauge*
Size D-3/3.25 mm crochet hook

NOTIONS
Yarn needle

MEASUREMENTS
Circumference at brim (unstretched) 21";
length from edge of turned brim to tip (excluding tassel) 14"

GAUGE
9 sts = 2 inches / 5 rows = 1"

SPECIAL STITCH
Left Twist (LT): Knit second stitch on left-hand needle through back loop; leave on needle. Knit first stitch on left-hand needle normally; drop both sts from needle.

CROCHET STITCHES USED
Chain (ch)
Single crochet (sc)

PATTERN

HAT

Cast on 8 sts.

Row 1: Purl.

Row 2: Knit.

Row 3: Purl.

Row 4: *Inc 1 st in first st, k1; repeat from * to end. (12 sts)

Rows 5–7: Repeat rows 1–3.

Row 8: *Inc 1 st in first st, k2; repeat from * to end. (16 sts)

Rows 9–11: Repeat rows 1–3.

Row 12: *Inc 1 st in first st, k3; repeat from * to end. (20 sts)

Row 13: Purl.

Row 14: *Inc 1 st in first st, k4; repeat from * to end. (24 sts)

Row 15: Purl.

Row 16: *Inc 1 st in first st, k5; repeat from * to end. (28 sts)

Row 17: Purl.

Row 18: *Inc 1 st in first st, k6; repeat from * to end. (32 sts)

Row 19: Purl.

Row 20: *Inc 1 st in first st, k7; repeat from * to end. (36 sts)

Row 21: Purl.

Row 22: *Inc 1 st in first st, k8; repeat from * to end. (40 sts)

Row 23: Purl.

Row 24: *Inc 1 st in first st, k9; repeat from * to end. (44 sts)

Row 25: Purl.

Row 26: *Inc 1 st in first st, k10; repeat from * to end. (48 sts)

Row 27: Purl.

Row 28: *Inc 1 st in first st, k11; repeat from * to end. (52 sts)

Row 29: Purl.

Row 30: *Inc 1 st in first st, k12; repeat from * to end. (56 sts)

Row 31: Purl.

Row 52: *Inc 1 st in first st, k13; repeat from * to end. (60 sts)

Row 53: Purl.
Row 54: *Inc 1 st in first st, k14; repeat from * to end. (64 sts)
Row 55: Purl.
Row 56: *Inc 1 st in first st, k15; repeat from * to end. (68 sts)
Row 57: Purl.
Row 58: *Inc 1 st in first st, k16; repeat from * to end. (72 sts)
Row 59: Purl.
Row 60: *Inc 1 st in first st, k17; repeat from * to end. (76 sts)
Row 61: Purl.
Row 62: *Inc 1 st in first st, k18; repeat from * to end. (80 sts)
Row 63: Purl.

Row 64: *Inc 1 st in first st, k19; repeat from * to end. (84 sts)
Row 65: Purl.
Row 66: *Inc 1 st in first st, k20; repeat from * to end. (88 sts)
Row 67: Purl.
Work even in stockinette stitch until piece measures 14 inches from beginning; end with p row.
Next row: *K43, inc 1 st in next st; repeat from * to end. (90 sts)

BRIM
Row 1: *K1, LT; repeat from * to end.
Row 2: Purl.
Rows 3–14: Repeat rows 1 and 2.
Bind off.

TASSEL
Wind yarn 40 times around a 6-inch piece of cardboard. Tie at one end securely, leaving the ends of the tying yarn long to attach the tassel to the hat; cut all the strands on other end of the tassel. Trim ends evenly.

TASSEL CUP
With crochet hook, ch 3. Join with a sl st to form a ring.
Round 1: Work 6 sc through center of ring.
Round 2: Work 2 sc in back loop of each st. (12 sts)
Round 3: *Work 1 sc in first st, 2 sc in next st. Repeat from * around. (18 sts)
Rounds 4–8: Sc in each st around.
Fasten off.

FINISHING
Sew back seam of hat. Place cup over end of tassel, drawing ends of tying yarn through the hole in the top. Attach tassel to point of hat. If desired, sew the folded-over portion of the hat to the brim. Weave in ends.

First-Day-of-School Beret

SKILL LEVEL

EASY

This classic design is adorable on younger kids but stylish enough to satisfy older fashionistas. Trim it with a knitted tab, as shown here, or add a pompom for a more playful look.

3
Light

YARN
Knit Picks Swish DK (100% superwash merino wool; 123 yd; 50 g) in bordeaux (2 skeins)

NEEDLES
1 set size 7/4.5 mm straight needles *or size needed to obtain gauge*

NOTIONS
Yarn needle

MEASUREMENTS
Small: Circumference at brim (unstretched) 15$\frac{1}{2}$"; diameter 8$\frac{1}{2}$"

Large: Circumference at brim (unstretched) 17"; diameter 9$\frac{1}{2}$"

GAUGE
In garter stitch, 5 sts / 8 rows = 1"

PATTERN

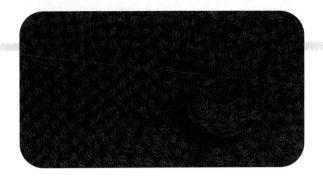

Instructions are for small (2–4 years) with instructions for large (6–8 years) in brackets.

Cast on 10 sts.
Row 1: Inc. 1 st in each st. (20 sts)
Row 2: Knit.
Row 3: (K1, inc 1 st in next st) 10 times. (30 sts)
Row 4: Knit.
Row 5: (K2, inc 1 st in next st) 10 times. (40 sts)
Row 6: Knit.
Row 7: (K3, inc 1 st in next st) 10 times. (50 sts)
Rows 8–10: Knit.
Row 11: (K4, inc 1 st in next st) 10 times. (60 sts)
Row 12: Knit.
Row 13: (K5, inc 1 st in next st) 10 times. (70 sts)
Rows 14–16: Knit.
Row 17: (K6, inc 1 st in next st) 10 times. (80 sts)
Row 18: Knit.
Row 19: (K7, inc 1 st in next st) 10 times. (90 sts)
Rows 20–22: Knit.
Row 23: (K8, inc 1 st in next st) 10 times. (100 sts)
Row 24: Knit.
Row 25: (K9, inc 1 st in next st) 10 times. (110 sts)
Rows 26–28: Knit.
Row 29: (K10, inc 1 st in next st) 10 times. (120 sts)
Row 30: Knit.
Row 31: (K 11, inc 1 st in next st) 10 times. (130 sts)
For size 6–8 years only:
Rows 32–34: Knit.
Row 35: (K12, inc 1 st in next st) 10 times. (140 sts)
    Proceed to row 32.
Rows 32–44 {36–48}: Knit.
Row 45 {49}: *K3, k2tog. Repeat from * to end of
    row. (104 sts {112 sts})
Row 46 {50}: Knit.
Row 47 {51}: *K2, k2tog. Repeat from * to end of
    row. (78 sts {84 sts})

Row 48 {52}: Knit.
Row 49 {53}: Knit.
Row 50 {54}: Purl.
Rows 51–55 {55–59}: Repeat rows 49–50 {53–54},
    ending with a knit row.
Row 56 {60}: Knit.
Rows 57–60 {61–64}: Repeat rows 49–50 {53–54}
    twice.
Bind off loosely enough to allow this edge to fit
    around head.

TAB
Cast on 3 sts and work 2 inches in stockinette
    stitch. Bind off.

FINISHING
Sew back seam. Turn the bottom portion of the
headband to the inside of the hat and sew into
position. Sew tab to top of beret.

Reindeer Ski Cap

SKILL LEVEL

EXPERIENCED

This fun, festive cap for the holidays can be made in more neutral colors—as shown here— or dialed all the way up in red and green. If you have a hunting enthusiast in your life, you could make this hat in blaze orange and black to fit a different kind of season.

3

Light

YARN
Knit Picks Swish DK (100%
superwash merino wool;
123 yd; 50 g)

A: white (2 skeins)
B: dusk (2 skeins)

NEEDLES
1 set size 8/5 mm circular or double-pointed
    needles *or size needed to obtain gauge*

MEASUREMENTS
Circumference at brim (unstretched) 22";
    height (with brim turned up) 8"

GAUGE
11 sts = 2" / 6 rows = 1"

PATTERN

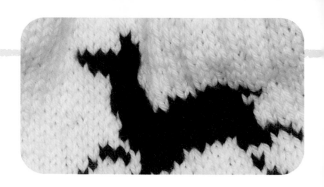

With color A, cast on 112 sts. Join to work in round, being careful not to twist sts.

Work in k1, p1 ribbing for 2½ inches. Working in stockinette st, follow the chart for 30 rounds.

Work 2 more rounds stockinette st.

CROWN SHAPING

Round 1: P1, *(k1, p1) 5 times, k1, sl2, k1, psso. Repeat from * to last 13 sts; (k1, p1) 5 times, k1, p2 tog. (97 sts)

Round 2: K1, *(k1, p1) 5 times, k2. Repeat from * to last 12 sts; (k1, p1) 6 times.

Round 3: (P1, k1) 6 times, *k2, (p1, k1) 5 times. Repeat from * to last st, p1.

Round 4: Repeat round 2.

Round 5: K2tog, *(p1, k1) 4 times, p1, sl2, k1, psso. Repeat from * to last 11 sts; (p1, k1) 4 times, p1, k2tog. (81 sts)

Rounds 6–8: Work in k1, p1 rib.

Round 9: P2tog, *(k1, p1) 3 times, k1, sl2, k1, psso. Repeat from * to last 9 sts; (k1, p1) 3 times, k1, p2tog. (65 sts)

Round 10: P1, *(k1, p1) 3 times, k2. Repeat from * to last 8 sts; (k1, p1) 4 times.

Round 11: (P1, k1) 4 times, *k2, (p1, k1) 3 times. Repeat from * to last st, p1.

Round 12: Repeat round 10.

Round 13: K2tog, *(p1, k1) twice), p1, sl2, k1, psso. Repeat from * to last 7 sts, (p1, k1) twice, p1, k2tog. 49 sts.

Round 14: Work in k1, p1 rib.

Round 15: P2tog, *sl2, k1, psso. Repeat from * to last 2 sts, p2tog. (17 sts)

Round 16: *Sl2, k1, psso. Repeat from * to last 2 sts, p2tog.

Break yarn. Draw end through remaining 6 sts and fasten off securely. Weave in ends.

Trim with a pompom.

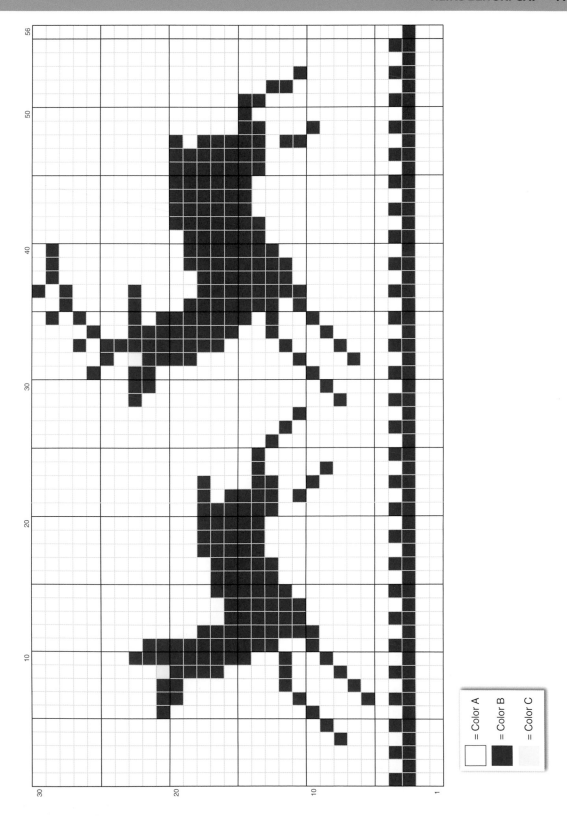

= Color A

= Color B

= Color C

Slouchy Newsboy Cap

SKILL LEVEL

EXPERIENCED

The extra elements on this hat may look intimidating to make, but the great retro look of the finished piece is well worth the extra effort. The main body of the hat is knitted flat and seamed in the back, and the brim and band are knitted separately and sewn on afterward. Made in chunky yarn, this hat knits up quickly!

YARN
Plymouth Encore Chunky
Tweed (75% acrylic, 22% wool,
3% rayon; 143 yd; 3.5 oz/100 g)
in #T134 (orange) (2 skeins)

NEEDLES
1 set size 7/4.5 mm straight needles *or size
needed to obtain gauge*

NOTIONS
Stiff cardboard or plastic (such as a
notebook cover)
Duct tape
Yarn needle

MEASUREMENTS
Circumference at brim 20"; diameter at widest
point (with hat laid flat) 11"

GAUGE
4 stitches/6 rows in stockinette stitch = 1"

PATTERN

BODY OF HAT

Cast on 93 sts.

Row 1: K1, *p1, k1, repeat from * to end.

Row 2: P1, *k1, p1, repeat from * to end.

Rows 3–4: Repeat rows 1–2.

Row 5: K1, *k2tog, repeat from * to end.

Row 6: P1, *M1, p1, repeat from * to end.

Row 7: *K1, kfb, k1, repeat from * to end. (124 sts)

Row 8: Purl.

Row 9: K1, *k2tog, repeat from * until last stitch, k1.

Row 10: P2, *M1, p1, repeat from * to end.

Row 11: Knit.

Row 12: Purl.

Rows 13–32: Repeat rows 9–12.

SHAPING FOR CROWN

Rows 33–34: Repeat rows 9–10.

Row 35: K2, *ssk, k16, k2tog, repeat from * to last two stitches, k2.

Row 36: Repeat row 12.

Rows 37–38: Repeat rows 9–10.

Row 39: K2, *ssk, k14, k2tog, repeat from * to last two stitches, k2.

Row 40: Repeat row 12.

Rows 41–42: Repeat rows 9–10.

Row 43: K2, *ssk, k12, k2tog, repeat from * to last two stitches, k2.

Row 44: Repeat row 12.

Rows 45–46: Repeat rows 9–10.

Row 47: K2, *ssk, k10, k2tog, repeat from * to last two stitches, k2.

Row 48: Repeat row 12.

Rows 49–50: Repeat rows 9–10.

Row 51: K2, *ssk, k8, k2tog, repeat from * to last two stitches, k2.

Row 52: Repeat row 12.

Rows 53–54: Repeat rows 9–10.

Row 55: K2, *ssk, k6, k2tog, repeat from * to last two stitches, k2.

Row 56: Repeat row 12.

Rows 57–58: Repeat rows 9–10.

Row 59: K2, *ssk, k1, k2tog, k1, k2tog, repeat from * to last two stitches, k2.

Row 60: Repeat row 12.

Row 61: K1, *k2tog, repeat from * to end.

Row 62: P2tog across.

Cut yarn, draw end through rem sts, and fasten off. Sew back seam.

BAND

Cast on 4 stitches, work in garter stitch (knit plain every row) until work measures 10 inches. Bind off.

BRIM

Cast on 41 stitches.
Row 1: K2tog, k to last 2 stitches, k2tog.
Row 2: Purl.
Row 3: K2tog, k9, turn.
Row 4: With yarn behind work, slip first st off right hand needle on to left hand needle. Bring yarn to front of work and slip the slipped st back onto right hand needle. When turning, always slip and wrap first stitch from right hand needle in this manner to prevent a hole. Purl to last 2 st, p2tog.
Row 5: K2tog, k2, turn.
Row 6: P1, p2tog.
Row 7: K2tog, k to last 2 stitches, k2tog.
Row 8: P2tog, p8, turn.
Row 9: K to last 2 st, k2tog.
Row 10: P2tog, p1, turn.
Row 11: K2tog.
Row 12: P2tog, p to last 2 stitches, p2tog.
Row 13: K2tog, k to last 2 stitches, k2tog.
Rows 14–19: Repeat rows 12–13 three times (13 stitches remaining).
Row 20: Pfb, p to last stitch, pfb.
Row 21: Kfb, k to last stitch, kfb.
Rows 22-26: Repeat rows 20 and 21 two and a half times, ending with row 20 (27 stitches remaining).
Row 27: Kfb, k5, turn.
Row 28: P to last stitch, pfb.
Row 29: Kfb, k2, turn.
Row 30: P to last stitch, pfb.
Row 31: Kfb, k to last stitch, kfb.
Row 32: Pfb, p7, turn.
Row 33: K to last stitch, kfb.
Row 34: Pfb, p4, turn.
Row 35: K to last stitch, kfb.
Row 36: Pfb, p to last stitch, pfb.
Row 37: Knit.
Row 38: Pfb, p to last stitch, pfb.
Bind off.

FINISHING

Sew shaped edges of brim together. Cut a piece of cardboard the same shape as the brim; for added durability, wrap this piece in duct tape. Place this piece inside the brim and sew the seam along the long edge. Sew the brim to the front of the hat. Sew the band to the hat at each end of the brim. Weave in all ends.

Tasseled Hood

The slipped-stitch pattern used in this combination hat and scarf creates a beautifully thick, stretchy fabric that looks like ribbing from far off but is much softer. Made in one long rectangle and sewn up at the end, this hood is very easy to adjust to any size.

YARN

Cascade Yarns Cascade 220
(100% Peruvian highland wool;
164 yd/150 m; 50 g/1.75 oz) in
azure (3 skeins)

NEEDLES

1 set size 2/2.75 mm straight
needles *or size needed to
obtain gauge*

NOTIONS

Yarn needle

MEASUREMENTS

Length of one side of scarf from top of head
to end of scarf 26"

GAUGE

In pattern, 4 sts = 1" / 11 rows = 2"

PATTERN

Cast on 46 sts.
Row 1: Knit.
Row 2: K2, *yo, sl 1, k1; repeat from * to last 2 sts; k2.

In this pattern, always slip stitches purlwise, holding the yarn in back of the work.

Row 3: K2, *yo, sl 1, k2tog; repeat from * to last 2 sts; k2.
Repeat row 3 until work measures 58 inches; bind off.

TASSEL
Wrap the yarn around a piece of cardboard 6 inches wide 150 times. Tie a short piece of yarn securely around strands at one end; cut strands at opposite end. Fold the bundle of strands in half and tie another short piece of yarn around the whole bundle about 1 inch from the center tie.

FINISHING
Fold piece in half and sew along one side for 7 inches from the fold. Turn the piece inside out so the seam is on the inside. Sew the tassel to the end of the hood. Weave in ends.

Jack-Be-Nimble Stocking Cap

SKILL LEVEL

EASY

Little ones will love this playful stocking cap. The hat is knitted flat on 2 needles, then transferred to double-pointed needles for the I-cord at the end. If you prefer, you can knit the last 10 rows in stockinette stitch on the straight needles and seam the I-cord up with the rest of the hat. Or you can knit the whole thing on double-pointed needles (just remember to knit the even rows instead of purling).

49

3
Light

YARN
Knit Picks Swish DK (100% superwash merino wool; 123 yd; 50 g) in carrot (1 skein) and cornmeal (1 skein)

NEEDLES
1 set size 6/4 mm straight needles *or size needed to obtain gauge*
2 size 6/4 mm double-pointed needles

NOTIONS
Yarn needle

MEASUREMENTS
Circumference at brim (unstretched) 13"; turned brim to tip 17"

GAUGE
5 sts / 7 rows = 1"

PATTERN

With color A, cast on 92 sts and work 4 inches in k2, p2 ribbing. Change to color B.

Row 1: Knit.

Row 2: Purl.

Rows 3–8: Repeat rows 1–2.

Row 9: *K21, k2tog. Repeat from * to end of row. (88 sts)

Row 10: Purl.

Row 11: Knit.

Row 12: Purl.

Row 13: *K20, k2tog. Repeat from * to end of row. (84 sts)

Rows 14–16: Repeat rows 10–12.

Row 17: *K19, k2tog. Repeat from * to end of row. (80 sts)

Rows 18–20: Repeat rows 10–12.

Row 21: *K18, k2tog. Repeat from * to end of row. (76 sts)

Rows 22–24: Repeat rows 10–12.

Row 25: *K17, k2tog. Repeat from * to end of row. (72 sts)

Rows 26–28: Repeat rows 10–12.

Row 29: *K16, k2tog. Repeat from * to end of row. (68 sts)

Rows 30–32: Repeat rows 10–12.

Row 33: *K15, k2tog. Repeat from * to end of row. (64 sts)

Rows 34–36: Repeat rows 10–12.

Row 37: *K14, k2tog. Repeat from * to end of row. (60 sts)

Rows 38–40: Repeat rows 10–12.

Row 41: *K13, k2tog. Repeat from * to end of row. (56 sts)

Rows 42–44: Repeat rows 10–12.

Row 45: *K12, k2tog. Repeat from * to end of row. (52 sts)

Rows 46–48: Repeat rows 10–12.

Row 49: *K11, k2tog. Repeat from * to end of row. (48 sts)

Rows 50–52: Repeat rows 10–12.

Row 53: *K10, k2tog. Repeat from * to end of row. (44 sts)

Rows 54–56: Repeat rows 10–12.

Row 57: *K9, k2tog. Repeat from * to end of row. (40 sts)

Rows 58–60: Repeat rows 10–12.

Row 61: *K8, k2tog. Repeat from * to end of row. (36 sts)

Rows 62–64: Repeat rows 10–12.

Row 65: *K7, k2tog. Repeat from * to end of row. (32 sts)

Rows 66–68: Repeat rows 10–12.

Row 69: *K6, k2tog. Repeat from * to end of row. (28 sts)

Rows 70–72: Repeat rows 10–12.

Row 73: *K5, k2tog. Repeat from * to end of row. (24 sts)

Rows 74–76: Repeat rows 10–12.

Row 77: *K4, k2tog. Repeat from * to end of row. (20 sts)

Rows 78–80: Repeat rows 10–12.

Row 81: *K3, k2tog. Repeat from * to end of row. (16 sts)

Rows 82–84: Repeat rows 10–12.

Row 85: *K2, k2tog. Repeat from * to end of row. (12 sts)

Rows 86–88: Repeat rows 10–12.

Row 89: *K1, k2tog. Repeat from * to end of row. (8 sts)

Rows 90–92: Repeat rows 10–12.

Row 93: *K2tog. Repeat from * to end of row. (4 sts)

Transfer remaining 4 sts to a double-pointed needle. Create an I-cord as follows: Knit all stitches on needle. *Do not turn.* Switch right-hand needle to left hand and pull sts to other end of needle. Pull yarn firmly around behind work, ready to knit into the first st again (1 row of I-cord completed).

Work I-cord for 10 rows. On 11th row (row 104 counting from beginning of color B), k2tog twice. Past first st over second st; cut yarn and pull end through remaining st to fasten.

FINISHING

With color A, make a tassel: Wind the yarn around a 5-inch piece of cardboard 30 times. Slide the wrapped yarn off the cardboard and slide another piece of color A through and tie tightly around all strands, leaving ends long for now. About 1 inch lower, tie a second piece of color A firmly around the outside of the whole bunch of strands. At the bottom end of the tassel, cut the yarn in the middle so the strands from both sides end up about the same length.

Sew side seam of hat. Place the seam on the brim (the section in color A) on the outside so it is concealed when the brim is folded up. Using the long yarn ends at the top of the tassel, attach the tassel to the end of the I-cord portion of the hat. Weave in ends.

Paper Doll
Snow Hat

SKILL LEVEL

◼◼◼◼

EXPERIENCED

Like a chain of paper dolls, tiny figures, hand in hand ring this Fair-Isle hat. As always with Fair-Isle colorwork, remember to carry the unused yarn loosely along the back of the work and twist it with the working yarn every few stitches so the fabric retains its stretch.

3
Light

YARN
100% wool DK yarn
A: teal (1 skein)
B: white (1 skein)
C: mustard (1 skein)

NEEDLES
1 set size 5/3.75 mm double-pointed or
circular needles *or size needed to obtain
gauge*

MEASUREMENTS
Circumference at brim (unstretched) 18"

GAUGE
8 sts in stockinette st = 1"

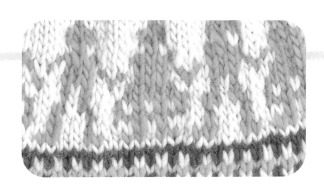

PATTERN

With color A, cast on 112 sts. Join to work in round, being careful not to twist sts.

Work in k1, p1 ribbing for 5 ½ inches. Change to color B and work two rounds in stockinette st. Continue to work in stockinette stitch, following the chart, for 26 rounds.

Round 27: *K11, sl 2, k1, psso; repeat from * around. (96 sts)

Rounds 28–30: Knit.

Round 31: *K9, sl 2, k1, psso; repeat from * around. (80 sts)

Rounds 32–34: Knit.

Round 35: *K7, sl2, k1, psso; repeat from * around. (64 sts)

Rounds 36–38: Knit.

Round 39: *K5, sl2, k1, psso; repeat from * around. (48 sts)

Round 40: Knit.

Round 41: (Sl2, k1, psso) around. (16 sts)

Round 42: K2tog 8 times. (8 sts)

Break yarn, draw end through rem sts, and fasten off. Weave in ends.

■ = Color 1
□ = Color 2
▨ = Color 3

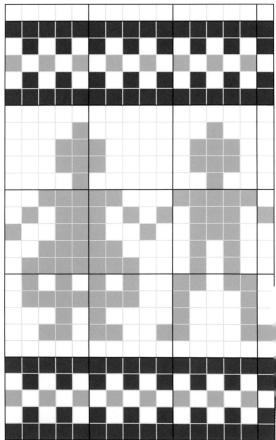

Red-Capped Robin Hat

This simple hat is a breeze to make! For a more casual, slouchy look, you could make it with bulky yarn and larger needles (and a larger gauge)—but even using worsted weight yarn, as shown here, you can knit this cap up in a weekend. Take care to work very loosely when knitting the ribbon and attaching it to the hat so the band of the hat retains its stretch.

Medium

YARN
Lion Brand Vanna's Choice
(100% acrylic; 170 yd/156 m;
3.5 oz/100 g) in cranberry
(1 skein)

NEEDLES
1 set size 6/4 mm straight needles *or size
needed to obtain gauge*

NOTIONS
Yarn needle

MEASUREMENTS
Circumference at brim (unstretched) 15"

GAUGE
4 sts / 5 rows = 1"

PATTERN

Cast on 54 sts.

Rows 1–15: Knit.

Row 16: *Kfb in next 5 sts, k1. Repeat from * to end of row. (99 sts)

Starting with a purl row, work in stockinette stitch until the piece measures 5 inches from the top of the garter stitch section.

Dec row 1: *K7, k2tog. Repeat from * to end of row.

Next row and all following alternate rows: Purl.

Dec row 2: *K3, k2tog. Repeat from * to last 3 sts. K3.

Dec row 3: *K1, k2tog. Repeat from * to end of row.

Dec row 4: K2tog across row.

Cut yarn and draw end through remaining sts.

RIBBON

Cast on 90 sts *loosely*. Bind off *loosely*. The resulting cord should measure 35 inches when stretched.

FINISHING

Sew back seam of hat. Baste around beret as illustrated and tie the ends in a soft knot. Weave in all ends.

Snowball Fight Hat

SKILL LEVEL

EASY

This thick, cozy hat will keep little ones' ears and cheeks warm even on the coldest day! Knit it in subtly variegated yarn, as shown here, or mix it up by adding stripes.

5
Bulky

YARN
Plymouth Encore Chunky
Colorspun (75% acrylic, 25%
wool; 143 yd; 100 g) in #7126

NEEDLES
1 set size 10½/6.5 mm straight needles *or size
needed to obtain gauge*

NOTIONS
Yarn needle
1 button (⅝" diameter)
Elastic (⅛" wide)

MEASUREMENTS
Circumference at brim (unstretched) 22"

GAUGE
7 sts / 10 rows = 2"

PATTERN

EARFLAPS
Cast on 3 sts.
Row 1: K1, inc in next st, k1. (4 sts)
Row 2: Knit.
Row 3: K1, inc in next 2 sts, k1. (6 sts)
Row 4: Knit.
Row 5: K1, inc in next st, k to last 2 sts, inc in next st, k1. (8 sts)
Row 6: Knit.
Rows 7–16: Repeat rows 5 and 6 five times. (18 sts after row 16)
Rows 17–18: Knit. †
Break off the yarn, leaving the stitches on the needle (or transfer to a scrap piece of yarn).
Make another earflap in the same way, but stop at † and go to the hat section of the pattern.

HAT
On same needle as second earflap, cast on 8 sts at end of last row; turn. (26 sts on needle)
Row 1: K26, cast on 20, k across 18 sts of first earflap, cast on 8. (72 sts)
Rows 2–8: Knit.
Row 9: Knit.
Row 10: K1, p to last st, k1.
Repeat rows 9 and 10 for 5 inches, finishing at the end of a row 10.

CROWN SHAPING
Row 1: [K4, k2tog] 12 times. (60 sts)
Row 2: Knit.
Row 3: [K3, k2tog] 12 times. (48 sts)
Row 4: Knit.
Row 5: [K2, k2tog] 12 times. (36 sts)
Row 6: Knit.
Row 7: [K1, k2tog] 12 times. (24 sts)
Row 8: Knit.
Row 9: [K2tog] 12 times. (12 sts)
Break off yarn, draw end through remaining sts, and fasten off securely.

FINISHING
Sew the back seam and weave in ends. Sew an elastic loop to the inside of the point of one earflap and a button to the outside of the point of each earflap.

Leaf Motif Cap

This hat is a bit of a challenge, with a body worked in a lace pattern and an assembly process of several steps. But such a lovely, unique hat deserves to be given a professional finish—and the results will not disappoint!

YARN
Knit Picks Capretta (80% fine merino wool, 10% cashmere, 10% nylon; 230 yd; 50 g) in harbor (1 skein)

NEEDLES
1 set size 2/2.75 mm double-pointed needles
or size needed to obtain gauge

NOTIONS
Sewing needle
Sewing thread
Grosgrain ribbon (1" wide)

MEASUREMENTS
Front band around face 13"

GAUGE
7 sts / 10 rows = 1"

PATTERN

BODY OF HAT

Cast on 8 sts. Join in round.

Round 1: *Yo, k1. Repeat from * to end of round. (16 sts; 4 on first needle, 4 on second needle, 8 on third needle)

Round 2: Knit.

Round 3: *Yo, k3, yo, k1 tbl. Repeat from * to end of round. (24 sts)

Round 4: Knit.

Round 5: *Yo, k5, yo, k1 tbl. Repeat from * to end of round. (32 sts)

Round 6: Knit.

Round 7: *Yo, k7, yo, k1 tbl. Repeat from * to end of round. (40 sts)

Round 8: Knit.

Round 9: *Yo, ssk, k2tog, yo, k1. Repeat from * to end of round. (40 sts)

Round 10: Knit.

Round 11: *K1, yo, k2tog, yo, k2. Repeat from * to end of round. (48 sts)

Round 12: Knit.

Round 13: *K2, yo, k1 tbl, yo, k3. Repeat from * to end of round. (64 sts)

Round 14: Knit.

Round 15: *K3, yo, k1 tbl, yo, k4. Repeat from * to end of round. (80 sts)

Round 16: Knit.

Round 17: *K4, yo, k1 tbl, yo, k5. Repeat from * to end of round. (96 sts)

Round 18: Knit.

Round 19: *K5, yo, k1 tbl, yo, k6. Repeat from * to end of round. (112 sts)

Round 20: Knit.

Round 21: *K6, yo, k1 tbl, yo, k7. Repeat from * to end of round. (128 sts; 32 on first needle, 32 on second needle, 64 on third needle)

Round 22: Knit.

Round 23: *Ssk, k4, yo, k3, yo, k4, k2tog, p1. Repeat from * to end of round. (128 sts)

Round 24: *K15, p1. Repeat from * to end of round.

Round 25: *Ssk, k3, yo, k5, yo, k3, k2tog, p1. Repeat from * to end of round. (128 sts)

Round 26: Repeat round 24.

Round 27: *Ssk, k2, yo, k7, yo, k2, k2tog, p1. Repeat from * to end of round. (128 sts)

Round 28: Repeat round 24.

Round 29: *Ssk, k1, yo, k9, yo, k1, k2tog, p1. Repeat from * to end of round. (128 sts)

Round 30: Repeat round 24.

Round 31: *Ssk, yo k11, yo, k2tog, p1. Repeat from * to end of round. (128 sts; 32 on first needle, 32 on second needle, 64 on third needle)

Round 32: Repeat round 24. Slip 1 st off each needle onto end of preceding needle.

Round 33: *Yo, k13, yo; sl 1, k2tog, psso. Repeat from * to end of round.

Round 34: *P1, k1 into the yo of previous round, k13, k1, p1 into the yo of the previous round, k1. Repeat from * to end of round. (144 sts; 36 on first needle, 36 on second needle, 72 on third needle)

Rounds 35–42: Knit.

Round 43: K11. Bind off next 13 sts. Knit to end of round, then on the 11 sts from the beginning of the round, k9, k2 tog. Turn. (130 sts)

End of rounds; hat is now worked in rows backwards and forwards.

Row 1: Bind off 2 sts pwise. Purl to last 2 sts, p2tog. (127 sts)

Row 2: Bind off 2 sts kwise. Knit to last 2 sts, k2tog. (124 sts)

Rows 3–12: Repeat rows 1 and 2. (94 sts at end of row 12)
Bind off.

BAND

With two needles cast on 12 sts. Work 14 inches even in stockinette st. Bind off.

BOW

Cast on 16 sts. Join in round. Knit even in round for 5 inches. Bind off.

FINISHING

Weave in all ends and block hat.

Turn under a $^3/_8$-inch hem along entire back edge of hat and sew into position.

Baste a piece of ribbon in the center of the wrong side of the band so that the ends of the ribbon come within $^1/_4$ inch of each end of the knitted band. Turn 2 sts of the long edges over the ribbon and sew into place. Place band along face edge of hat with one hemmed edge of the band just overlapping the bind-off edge of the hat and sew these edges together, leaving enough band at each end to fold underneath.

Sew another piece of ribbon $^1/_4$ inch from the edge along the back of the hat, hemming the ends over the seams on the face edge.

Approximately $^1/_2$ inch from each end of the band, make a loop (sewing it down over preexisting seams) to pass a bobby pin through when wearing the hat. This will keep the hat on.

Turn the ends of the bow inward to form a point at each end, and sew. Gather the center up slightly and sew it to the center of the bonnet, about $^1/_2$ inch from the edge.

Cozy Hood

SKILL LEVEL

INTERMEDIATE

This soft, toasty hat gives you plenty of room to customize to fit any child's personality. Subtle colors and wooden buttons, as shown here, give it a cute, feminine look. Another child might prefer bright, contrasting stripes or specialty buttons.

YARN
Lion Brand Wool-Ease
(80% acrylic, 20% wool;
197 yd/180 m; 3 oz/85 g)
A: rose heather (1 skein)
B: blush heather (1 skein)

NEEDLES
1 set size 7/4.5 mm straight needles *or size
needed to obtain gauge*

NOTIONS
Yarn needle
2 buttons ($5/8$" diameter)

MEASUREMENTS
$11\frac{1}{2}$" tall; neck circumference 10"
(unstretched)

GAUGE
9 sts = 2"; 6 rows = 1"

PATTERN

With A, cast on 72 sts.
Row 1: Knit.
Row 2: Purl.
Row 3: Knit. Join B.
Row 4: (With B) knit.
Row 5: Purl.
Row 6: Knit.
Row 7: P4, *inc 1 pwise, p8. Repeat from * to last 5 sts. Inc 1 st in next st; p4. (80 sts)
Row 8: With A, knit.
Row 9: Repeat row 8.
Row 10: Purl.
Row 11: Repeat row 8.
Row 12: With B, knit.
Row 13: Purl.
Row 14: Repeat row 12.
Row 15: Repeat row 13.
The purl stripe of three rows (color A) is the right side of the work.
Repeat rows 8–15 until there are 5 purl stripes on the right side of the work. After the last purl stripe, work rows 12 and 13, but do not work rows 14 and 15.
Row 38: With B, k25, k2tog, [k2, k2tog] 7 times, knit to end of row. (72 sts)
Rows 39–45: Repeat rows 8–14.
Row 46: K23, k2tog, [k1, k2tog] 8 times, knit to end of row. (63 sts)
Rows 47–53: Repeat rows 8–14.
Row 54: K21, [k2tog] 5 times, k1, [k2tog] 5 times, knit to end of row. (53 sts)
Rows 55–57: Repeat rows 8–10.
Bind off pwise.

NECKBAND

Fold work in half and sew back seam. With A, cast on 4 sts, then pick up and knit 58 sts along neck edge, then cast on 4 more sts. (66 sts)
Row 1: K4, *p2, k2. Repeat from * to last 6 sts, then p2, k4.

Row 2: K6, *p2, k2. Repeat from * to last 4 sts, then k4.
Row 3: Repeat row 1.
Row 4: Repeat row 2.
Row 5: K2, [yo, k2tog] for buttonhole, *p2, k2. Repeat from * to last 6 sts, p2, k4.
Row 6: Repeat row 2.
Rows 7–12: Repeat rows 1–6.
Continue to repeat rows 1 and 2 until ribbed border measures 3 inches in all. Bind off *loosely* in ribbing.

FINISHING

Weave in all ends. Sew buttons to neckband across from the buttonholes.

Highlander Beret

This unique five-sided beret with a subtle texture pattern is fun to make and wear. The pattern is given in two ways: Each row is written out as in a traditional pattern. But you may find the included stitch chart easier to follow.

Super Fine

YARN
Knit Picks Gloss (70% merino wool, 30% silk; 220 yd/50 g) in cranberry (1 skein)

NEEDLES
1 set size 3/3.25 mm circular or double-pointed needles *or size needed to obtain gauge*

MEASUREMENTS
Circumference at brim (unstretched) 20"; diameter 10"

GAUGE
8 sts / 10 rows = 1"

SPECIAL STITCH:
S1p2psso: Slip 1 stitch purlwise, purl 2 together, then pass the slipped stitch over the p2tog. Creates a centered 3-stitch decrease.

There are any number of increasing methods you could use in this pattern; knitting in the stitch below will give you the best results, however, since this increase is nearly invisible.

To knit in the stitch below: Lift the stitch below the next one, knitting it as if it's a stitch in your current row, then knit the next stitch on the left needle as normal.

PATTERN

Cast on 159 sts. Join to knit in the round, being
  careful not to twist stitches.
Round 1: *K1tbl, p1. Repeat from * to end of round.
Rounds 2–7: Repeat round 1.
Round 8: Repeat round 1, increasing 1 st in round.
  (160 sts)
Round 9: *P1, k1, p1, (k2, p2) 3 times, k2, p1, k2, (p2,
  k2) 3 times; repeat from * around.
Round 10: Repeat round 9.
Round 11: *P1, k1, p1, inc in next st, (k2, p2) 3 times,
  k3, (p2, k2) 3 times, inc in next st; repeat from *
  around.
Round 12: *P1, k1, p3, (k2, p2) 3 times, k3, (p2, k2) 3
  times, p2; repeat from * around.
Round 13: *P1, k1, p1, inc in next st, p2, (k2, p2) 3
  times, k1, (p2, k2) 3 times, p2, inc in next st;
  repeat from * around.
Round 14: *P1, k1, p1, (k2, p2) 4 times, k1, (p2, k2) 4
  times; repeat from * around.
Round 15: *P1, k1, p1, inc in next st, (k2, p2) 3 times,
  k2, p3, k2, (p2, k2) 3 times, inc in next st; repeat
  from * around.
Round 16: *P1, k1, p1, (p2, k2) 4 times, p3, (k2, p2) 4
  times; repeat from * around.
Round 17: *P1, k1, p1, inc in next st, (p2, k2) 4 times,
  p1, (k2, p2) 4 times, inc in next st; repeat from *
  around.
Round 18: *P1, k1, p1, (k2, p2) 4 times, k2, p1, k2, (p2,
  k2) 4 times; repeat from * around.
Round 19: *P1, k1, p1, inc in next st, (k2, p2) 4 times,
  k3, (p2, k2) 4 times, inc in next st; repeat from *
  around.
Round 20: *P1, k1, p3, (k2, p2) 4 times, k3, (p2, k2) 4
  times, p2; repeat from * around.
Round 21: *P1, k1, p1, inc in next st, (p2, k2) 4 times,
  p2, k1, p2, (k2, p2) 4 times, inc in next st; repeat
  from * around.
Round 22: *P1, k1, p1, (k2, p2) 5 times, k1, (p2, k2) 5
  times; repeat from * around.

Round 23: *P1, k1, p1, inc in next st, (k2, p2) 4 times,
  k2, p3, k2, (p2, k2) 4 times, inc in next st; repeat
  from * around.
Round 24: *P1, k1, p1, (p2, k2) 5 times, p3, (k2, p2) 5
  times; repeat from * around.
Round 25: *P1, k1, p1, k1, (p2, k2) 5 times, p1, (k2, p2)
  5 times, k1; repeat from * around.
Round 26: Repeat round 25.
Round 27: *P1, k1, p1, (k2, p2) 5 times, k3, (p2, k2) 5
  times; repeat from * around.
Round 28: Repeat round 27.
Round 29: *K2tog, p2tog, (k2, p2) 5 times, k1, (p2, k2)
  5 times, p1; repeat from * around.
Round 30: *K1, p1, (k2, p2) 5 times, k1, (p2, k2) 5
  times, p1; repeat from * around.
Round 31: *Ssk, p1, (k2, p2) 4 times, k2, p3, k2, (p2,
  k2) 4 times, p2; repeat from * around.
Round 32: *K1, p1, (k2, p2) 4 times, k2, p3, k2, (p2, k2)
  4 times, p2; repeat from * around.
Round 33: *Ssk, p1, (k2, p2) 4 times, k2, p1, k2, (p2,
  k2) 4 times, p1, p2tog; repeat from * around.
Round 34: *K1, p1, (k2, p2) 4 times, k2, p1, k2, (p2, k2)
  4 times, p2; repeat from * around.
Round 35: *Ssk, p1, (k2, p2) 4 times, k3, (p2, k2) 4
  times, p1, p2tog; repeat from * around.
Round 36: *K1, p1, (k2, p2) 4 times, k3, (p2, k2) 4
  times, p2; repeat from * around.
Round 37: *Ssk, p1, (k2, p2) 4 times, k1, (p2, k2) 4
  times, p1, p2tog; repeat from * around.
Round 38: *K1, p1, (k2, p2) 4 times, k1, (p2, k2) 4
  times, p2; repeat from * around.

Round 39: *Ssk, p1, (k2, p2) 3 times, k2, p3, k2, (p2, k2) 3 times, p1, p2tog; repeat from * around.

Round 40: *K1, p1, (k2, p2) 3 times, k2, p3, k2, (p2, k2) 3 times, p2; repeat from * around.

Round 41: *Ssk, p1, (k2, p2) 3 times, k2, p1, k2, (p2, k2) 3 times, p1, p2tog; repeat from * around.

Round 42: *K1, p1, (k2, p2) 3 times, k2, p1, k2, (p2, k2) 3 times, p2; repeat from * around.

Round 43: *Ssk, p1, (k2, p2) 3 times, k3, (p2, k2) 3 times, p1, p2tog; repeat from * around.

Round 44: *K1, p1, (k2, p2) 3 times, k3, (p2, k2) 3 times, p2; repeat from * around.

Round 45: *Ssk, p1, (k2, p2) 3 times, k1, (p2, k2) 3 times, p1, p2tog; repeat from * around.

Round 46: *K1, p1, (k2, p2) 3 times, k1, (p2, k2) 3 times, p2; repeat from * around.

Round 47: *Ssk, p1, (k2, p2) twice, k2, p3, k2, (p2, k2) twice, p1, p2tog; repeat from * around.

Round 48: *K1, p1, (k2, p2) twice, k2, p3, k2, (p2, k2) twice, p2; repeat from * around.

Round 49: *Ssk, p1, (k2, p2) twice, k2, p1, k2, (p2, k2) twice, p1, p2tog; repeat from * around.

Round 50: *K1, p1, (k2, p2) twice, k2, p1, k2, (p2, k2) twice, p2; repeat from * around.

Round 51: *Ssk, p1, (k2, p2) twice, k3, (p2, k2) twice, p1, p2tog; repeat from * around.

Round 52: *K1, p1, (k2, p2) twice, k3, (p2, k2) twice, p2; repeat from * around.

Round 53: *Ssk, p1, (k2, p2) twice, k1, (p2, k2) twice, p1, p2tog; repeat from * around.

Round 54: *K1, p1, (k2, p2) twice, k1, (p2, k2) twice, p2; repeat from * around.

Round 55: *Ssk, p1, k2, p2, k2, p3, k2, p2, k2, p1, p2tog; repeat from * around.

Round 56: *K1, p1, k2, p2, k2, p3, k2, p2, k2, p2; repeat from * around.

Round 57: *Ssk, p1, k2, p2, k2, p1, k2, p2, k2, p1, p2tog; repeat from * around.

Round 58: *K1, p1, k2, p2, k2, p1, k2, p2, k2, p2; repeat from * around.

Round 59: *Ssk, p1, k2, p2, k3, p2, k2, p1, p2tog; repeat from * around.

Round 60: *K1, p1, k2, p2, k3, p2, k2, p2; repeat from * around.

Round 61: *Ssk, p1, k2, p2, k1, p2, k2, p1, p2tog; repeat from * around.

Round 62: *K1, p1, k2, p2, k1, p2, k2, p2; repeat from * around.

Round 63: *Ssk, p1, k2, p3, k2, p1, p2tog; repeat from * around.

Round 64: *K1, p1, k2, p3, k2, p2; repeat from * around.

Round 65: *Ssk, p1, k1, sl 1 pwise, p2tog, psso, k1, p1, p2tog; repeat from * around.

Round 66: *Ssk, sl 1 pwise, p2tog, psso, p2tog; repeat from * around.

Break yarn, pull through remaining 15 sts, and fasten off.

Weave in ends.

	knit
●	purl
⅄	inc
λ	ssk
⅄	k2tog
⅄	p2tog
⟁	s1p2psso (sl 1 pw, p2tog, pass slipped stitch over)

Resources

SKILL LEVELS FOR KNITTING

1	◖☐☐▷	**Beginner**	Projects for first-time knitters using basic knit and purl stitches. Minimal shaping.
2	◖■☐▷	**Easy**	Projects using basic stitches, repetitive stitch patterns, simple color changes, and simple shaping and finishing.
3	◖■■▷	**Intermediate**	Projects with a variety of stitches, such as basic cables and lace, simple intarsia, double-pointed needles and knitting in the round needle techniques, mid-level shaping and finishing.
4	◖■■▶	**Experienced**	Projects using advanced techniques and stitches, such as short rows, Fair Isle, more intricate intarsia, cables, lace patterns, and numerous color changes.

This Standards & Guidelines booklet and downloadable symbol artwork are available at: **YarnStandards.com**

STANDARDS & GUIDELINES FOR CROCHET AND KNITTING

Standard Yarn Weight System

Categories of yarn, gauge ranges, and recommended needle and hook sizes

Yarn Weight Symbol & Category Names	0 Lace	1 Super Fine	2 Fine	3 Light	4 Medium	5 Bulky	6 Super Bulky
Type of Yarns in Category	Fingering 10 count crochet thread	Sock, Fingering, Baby	Sport, Baby	DK, Light Worsted	Worsted, Afghan, Aran	Chunky, Craft, Rug	Bulky, Roving
Knit Gauge Range* in Stockinette Stitch to 4 inches	33–40** sts	27–32 sts	23–26 sts	21–24 sts	16–20 sts	12–15 sts	6–11 sts
Recommended Needle in Metric Size Range	1.5–2.25 mm	2.25–3.25 mm	3.25–3.75 mm	3.75–4.5 mm	4.5–5.5 mm	5.5–8 mm	8 mm and larger
Recommended Needle U.S. Size Range	000 to 1	1 to 3	3 to 5	5 to 7	7 to 9	9 to 11	11 and larger
Crochet Gauge* Ranges in Single Crochet to 4 inch	32-42 double crochets**	21–32 sts	16–20 sts	12–17 sts	11–14 sts	8–11 sts	5–9 sts
Recommended Hook in Metric Size Range	Steel*** 1.6–1.4mm Regular hook 2.25 mm	2.25–3.5 mm	3.5–4.5 mm	4.5–5.5 mm	5.5–6.5 mm	6.5–9 mm	9 mm and larger
Recommended Hook U.S. Size Range	Steel*** 6, 7, 8 Regular hook B–1	B–1 to E–4	E–4 to 7	7 to I–9	I–9 to K–10½	K–10½ to M–13	M–13 and larger

* GUIDELINES ONLY: The above reflect the most commonly used gauges and needle or hook sizes for specific yarn categories.

** Lace weight yarns are usually knitted or crocheted on larger needles and hooks to create lacy, openwork patterns. Accordingly, a gauge range is difficult to determine. Always follow the gauge stated in your pattern.

*** Steel crochet hooks are sized differently from regular hooks--the higher the number, the smaller the hook, which is the reverse of regular hook sizing.

This Standards & Guidelines booklet and downloadable symbol artwork are available at: **YarnStandards.com**

Visual Index